KATHARINE TOWERS was born in London and now lives
in Derbyshire. She has published two poetry collections, both
with Picador. *The Floating Man* won the Seamus Heaney Centre
Prize and was shortlisted for the Jerwood-Aldeburgh First
Collection Prize and for the Ted Hughes Award for New Work in
Poetry. A poem from the collection, 'The Way We Go', appeared
as a Poem on the Underground and has been set to music by a
number of contemporary composers. Her second collection,
The Remedies, was shortlisted for the T. S. Eliot Prize.

Katharine's poems have been broadcast on Radio 3 and
Radio 4 and have appeared in several anthologies, as well
as in the *Guardian*, *Poetry Review* and *Poetry London*.
From 2016–2018 Katharine was Poet in Residence
at the Cloud Appreciation Society.

Katharine Towers

Oak

PICADOR

First published 2021 by Picador
an imprint of Pan Macmillan
6 Briset Street, London EC1M 5NR
EU representative: Macmillan Publishers Ireland Ltd, 1st Floor,
The Liffey Trust Centre, 117–126 Sheriff Street Upper, Dublin 1 D01 YC43
Associated companies throughout the world
www.panmacmillan.com

ISBN 978-1-5290-7842-8

1 3 5 7 9 8 6 4 2

A CIP catalogue record for this book is available from the British Library.

Printed and bound by CPI Group (UK) Ltd, Croydon, CR0 4YY

Visit **www.picador.com** to read more about all our books
and to buy them. You will also find features, author interviews and
news of any author events, and you can sign up for e-newsletters
so that you're always first to hear about our new releases.

for the good companions

Contents

Wae's me! Wae's me!
The acorn is not yet
Fallen from the tree
That's to grow the wood,
That's to make the cradle,
That's to rock the bairn,
That's to grow to a man,
That's to lay me.

The Rhyme of the Cauld Lad of Hilton,
– James Orchard Halliwell,
Popular Rhymes and Nursery Tales, 1849

I felt it happiness to be
Unknown, obscure and like a tree
In woodland peace and privacy.

– John Clare

1

this is not chaos
but a small change in our green midst
which shall not wreak havoc
nor shall it bring down curses or disaster
nor cause the seasons to go backwards
nor cause the weathers to upend

this is not chaos but a small change
afoot in the field's low ebb

such things are their own happening
and may not be our concern
we being the ones who were here first
and are therefore disposed to take the long view

this is not a moment for foretelling
a magnificent woe
but for speaking of a small
difference in our bright green midst
which may well come to something

and so we say once upon a time

after a mast year
an inkling like
the thought of a thought

far from the green skirts of the wood
an escapee acorn
can't contain itself

lacking something that's upwards
and something that's downwards
though neither knows what is lacked

(they'll know when they get to it)

no need for this broken old suitcase
which has been stepped out of
like a magician's box is stepped out of

something is moving
up through the dark and down through the dark
with a creaking you wouldn't believe how loud

surely it must hurt

tiny white wavering frond
tiny quivering foot

it's tempting to ask what if
Wind had not rattled so hard at the tree
Jay had not been called away across the field
Rain had not softened the blows
Earth had not agreed to pocket
this one for keeps

tiny white wavering frond
tiny quivering foot

wend your way lightwards
wend your way darkwards

tropic meaning *tending to turn*
without thought or desire

and here you are
poor wee thing
one foot down
flapping your new green wings

infant meaning *one not able to speak*
not meaning not able to shake
in the breeze not meaning
not able to muster a leaf the colour of ?

think of the green you sometimes see in art
but don't have a word for
you might say *it's too green*
not like real grass

if you look at an oakling's new leaf
you might say *it's the green*
I saw in a painting

a leaf must live a few hours in the world
before its colour will fit into language

origami
backwards

another leaf
uncomplicates

sunlight
irons it all out

O oakling!
addicted to water and light
and to shaking

why do you call to mind a paper
cocktail umbrella
perfect and useless

cranesbill orchid clover
sorrel plantain daisy
thistle knapweed dock

you can barely see an oakling
amid a meadow's fruitless waving
the quiet one getting on

without a fuss
like the kid in the corner
who's good at maths

bird's-foot trefoil
a little yellow purse
not much of a companion

and doesn't it make you sad
the flowers and trees
left out in the dark

the meadow grey under the moon
like a bleached reef
but very much not dead

in fact fending for itself
like the clean white owl
brushing across the grasses

     shhhh

        shhhh

           shhhh

a sapling meaning *one who's young*
slender as a greyhound

the trunk of a sapling is easily broken
under this or that thoughtless heel
or can be snapped off in jaws

a sapling isn't altogether sure
therefore keeps it simple

if in doubt
put everything
into up

2

it is not for us to read out loud
from the book of the future
but remember we are not stones

we have a mother's arms made for sorrow
a mother's mouth for speaking into the ear
of one who will not care to listen

when we mention how a certain hardness
must be grown and henceforth worn like a fine suit
equal to rude weathers and to kindly weathers

think of the throes of fortune or luck
which cause one to be trodden down and one
to muster itself and set foot

to take hold in the world
O think what must be garnered
what must be held in abeyance

a schoolboy throws his cap into a hedge
he squishes a slug to see what's inside
wears scabs on his knees like sewn-on badges
and doesn't care

a schoolboy stalks invisible creatures hiding
in traffic and over the edges of cliffs
for did a schoolboy ever heed a warning

a schoolboy keeps a beetle in a tin
kicks a stone for fun
takes a running jump

a schoolboy whispers in another schoolboy's ear
thinks he is *it*
thinks school is his own private fiefdom
or thinks it is where he will suffer in silence
for ever and ever amen

an example of a schoolboy error
rushing at things

an oakling must learn
some things need time

imagine a ripe old age
and think what it takes

an example of a schoolboy error
saying fuck that

a schoolboy hates rules but
here are the rules of ramification

trunk begets branch and branch begets
twig and twig begets twig begets twig

and each remembers the angle
that's needed to share out the wind

if this sounds like a lesson
in drawing it's not

and then there's the business
of twisting and kinking to wriggle

to where there's room for a new one
contortions by no means elegant

but all the same
smart

things to crow about

more leaves bodying forth
the manner in which they flutter
a resolve in the inner woody cells
and underneath the makings
of more than a toehold
the makings of making a stand

a sturdiness like a trumpet
sounding after the strings

although

a notch in the bark
the size of a wink
and it's only a matter of time

weakness gets noticed
by the ones you least want
(and whose strength lies in numbers)

a wound is like a dinner bell
FIRST COME FIRST SERVED

to flourish meaning *to flower*
to grow undaunted
able to seal up a trouble

and make of it a relic
like a socket
without an eye in it

if someone comes later and traces
the shape of the notch or nick with a finger
the oak will remember

a vague far-off pain
but never the truth
of the cut to the quick

a young oak is awkward of limb
and is easily swivelled
and swayed by the wind

which will tug
at the gangly branches
to see what is let go

with a *see-if-I-care*
and thrown away
like a textbook or satchel

and the young oak will learn
from the wind's unkind
pullings and pokings

that you must choose your battles
therefore beware the whip hand
this particular day in November

one brown leaf rips off
        one leaf twists and holds on
            as for the rest

3

it is also true
that if there is not love
there is no real story

and although we are old we remember
the madcap chapters of love
which we would wish upon anyone

still we are almost afraid to speak of it
there being more than enough meddlers
and trouble is never far away from love

for love is a juncture
at which a life may thoughtlessly
hurtle off

the heart being mainly
a cheerful muscle

such a thrill
when a bird comes

and a skinny branch
accepts his scant weight

it's only Robin
quite ordinary

all the same
a glory

the oak has reached the age of a lover
meaning *one who delights*
in a bird on a branch in spring

stupid to think an oak
could be in love
with a bird
but

an oak is not an iceberg
the oak you don't see
is not a dreadful undertow

an oak is two

and each needs the other
as the young man staring into a pond
needs what he sees in the water

and each loves the other
as the young man staring up from a pond
loves what he sees leaning over

I have three loves
Three loves have me

Without three loves
O what would I be

(and this is the song of the little oak tree)

regarding the first true love of an oak
which is Light

a tree will always mention the sun
in its manner of growing
for who won't mention too much
the one that they love

like a quirk of the tongue
which can't help curling
to make the shape of the name of the lover

thus an oak on its own in a field
will form itself into a dome

making of the sun a god
and of its leaves a worshipful company

regarding the second true love of an oak
which is Air

all day the leaves
gulp gulp
busy with a verb

a breeze rattles through the twigs
and might speak in passing
of the sea or a straight-sided hill

or a river with a swerve in it
this or that elsewhere
which Air carries in its teeth like the past

a tree must catch what it can before dark
when it will giantly exhale
like a whale spouting

regarding the third true love of an oak which is Rain

an oak in summer has a serious thirst
put your ear to the trunk
to hear water moving against gravity
up from the great sinker root
like an underground engine
droning and churning

or Rain is quickly passed from leaf to leaf
like a game of whispers

and Rain will dribble down the trunk
along the narrow twisty lanes
to end in dark

and Rain will wash an oak tree clean
and the oak will hang out its leaves to dry
and the leaves will show forth
their perfect tiny geographies

and behold the young oak in winter
wearing bristles of ice
like a jagged coat
slightly fierce or affronted

although the heart in its deeps
is not frozen

the heartwood is soft
and is beating

4

and it is also true that without
a great battle there is no real story

and although we will not point up
to a comet or to a raven
hunched on a church roof

still we must speak of danger
which has a way of rushing in
like a downpour or a cold wind

we must tell of how a schoolboy
will quickly make of himself
a brave fighter
and of what then befalls

if we were mothers
we would surely be weeping
but from this far edge we see only
small brandishings of weapons
and local smoke rising
from a burnt village

alas it is for us
to look on without speaking
and feel as little as we can

not yet mighty
but an oak that's grown and is
for want of a better word

complete
in all its oakish parts
and ready for the battle

soldier meaning *one who is paid with a gold coin*
not meaning anything brave

although
there may be no great battle

simply a reversal of fortune
such as a case of wrong weather

and if there is drought
the sinker root will try the usual ploys
the oak will plead

but useless to ask the parched earth
which is no stranger to patience
the oak must thirst

or if there is flood
the oak will find itself far out at sea
amid the meadow it grew out of

and will fill up to bulging
like a giant syringe

and will be troubled
by a fear of drowning

or if the oak breathes
long and deep
of poisoned air

it will find itself become
a secret archive
of all the things
that went wrong

an oak is a long book
in which are set down
the many mistakes
and misdemeanours

and these private writings
are a catalogue of woe

and an oak that's beset
by bad luck or bad thoughts
will quickly or slowly
forget about thriving

and will suffer galls and sores
and from its trunk weep
a bitter black treacle

and the twigs at the top
will forget about leaves
and the branches
forget about twigs

until the oak is simplified
into strengthlessness

and so begin
the countless tiny torments of an oak
which must not be succumbed to

and the first may be
the oak splendour beetle
more beautiful than it needs to be

a bright blue jewel
wearing on its back
a shimmer like a fish

the beetles dig dig
making of the bark
a map of corridors

then strip off the leaves
one by one by one by one

and the second may be
the oak processionary moth

which loves a long walk
(a long walk is a long feast)

the oak will feel
a gigantic itch

grub after grub
is boring a hole in the bark

off they go nose-to-tail
for a day of exploring

(forming a black and white swirl
like an op art drawing of panic)

imagine how many
tiny hairs and tiny mouths

and after many seasons
an oak will want only

to be left alone
to seek within itself

the mettle of a soldier
and an oak will

dress its wounds
and bandage up its scars

for a soldier is one
who will limp home

and will not wish
to be asked about the war

come back after years
to find an oak in its middle age
beleaguered and proud

like the tatters of an old banner
stuck into the ground
where something once was won

and the oak will have accrued
a certain unarguable staunchness

and the oak will be oh
so tremendously weary

5

this is the time in our story
for a letting go
the middle age of relinquishment

because a notice saying KEEP OUT
is of little use to one
whose life is sloping away

this is the time for an accommodation
to the many claims of others
which may be a form of meekness
or a form of goodness

although such questions are best
left to the gods of right/wrong

or to a weary old judge in pince-nez
and clean white ripples of curls
who will speak sweepingly
and without quibbles of doubt

and here is what happens next

the oak thinks
I think I am lonely

a meadow has nothing to say
a bird has no speech only song

Wind cares for no one
Rain stops for no one

the forest is looking forever
into itself and converses only in echoes

and best not to trust that old gossip the moon

yes, it is right to make room
for the many who depend
on oak's substance or form

substance being
bark's sweetness
leaves' tartness
and roots in their root-lair

form being
the little warm crannies
the dents and errors

shall we knock and see who's home?

here is oakmoss lichen
like a small grey beard

curly as miniature antlers
frondy like seaweed
earthy like fougère and chypre

(an oak in its lichen
resembles Miss Havisham
dressed in fine dust)

and here are oak milk-cap
with their smell of wet laundry
spending time en famille

they have nothing to say
being only listening devices

for it is meet and right
to sit here and wait

the word *humble* comes to mind

and here is Pip the Robin
who makes a quick house-call

and flicks up his tail
see you around

Woodpecker is a much better secret
to and fro like clockwork
close to the heartwood
although still not what you could call a friend

a green dash in the woodland
flying away from someone's bad joke
ha-ha
      ha-ha-ha

dipping through the branches
scuffling the forest floor and hoping
there'll be a few more years
before the bats move in

Monsieur Moustache
who toiled for days and nights
to hollow out this good home

which has all the curves and corners of home
and the softly rotted leaves of home
and the perfectly round opening to outside

think what will happen in here

think of the new pink tiny ones
made of mouths and elbows
squirming like grubs
no sooner grown and fun

than gone

leaving behind them
home's empty dark
the oak's slow slow-beating heart

still not a bad home
after a day rifling through the forest
trying to see the funny side

and then there's the ragged old owl
who comes once in a while
with his shivery cry

great big bird bumping into trees
who has a hankering
for this particular branch with a kink in it

brown owl blinks his brown eyes
thinks about mice
thinks about mice

it is right that an oak
offers a helping hand
setting the threads of milk-cap
roaming underground
scouting for others to tangle with

a mycologist would say
imagine it like hair growing
or like an intranet for urgent messages
or like someone looking for
a hook-up with a good match

and it's right that a lone oak
should speak with another
not as a confidant or friend
but as one of like need and mind
you scratch my back, I'll scratch yours

there may be a message
and such a message may take years

and it's right that an oak
should take its ease in the cold season
a fall of curling yellow leaves
like flimsy fortune fish
as if to say *dead one*

to rest meaning *to forget those things*
that might trouble an oak in its summer cups

meaning it's time to forget (let us say)
the question of beauty

pointless when twigs are the scribbles of a child
when branches have no reason
when a trunk is shown for the old hunchback it is

time to dig your heels into the hard ground

one time
a gale takes off a branch
the branch sighs and lies down
close to the beloved

one time
hailstones clatter in the dry twigs
like tiny boiled sweets and roll down
to comfort the poor branch that fell

one time
a storm rattles hard at Woodpecker's door
Woodpecker finds there is nothing funny in this
and buries his head in his green breast

one time
a storm arrives with bright white scissors
and makes tinder of a nearby sycamore
(which henceforth will be a symbol)

one time
a storm sloshes water
over the head of the oak which glitters
for an afternoon in seven-coloured beads

in between times
the oak stands

6

and there must always be money
which is ugly
and leaves its stink on our fingers

we would rather not speak of it
the way it flows on and on like a river

for money is not everything
and money is no object but an idea
and cannot be hidden away in a wardrobe
or under floorboards

still we would rather not speak of it
for it dirties the tongue
and trouble is never far away from money

what is accrued must be guarded
which is a great woe

and because there must always be money
we will hide our faces in the books of our hands
and fall into silence

a mast year is like when an orchestra
suddenly plays *fortissimo*
you have to cover your ears
for the splendour

the way the brass
gets right inside your chest
and makes a hollow doll of you

an oak puts everything into
50,000 little cups
each home to a beautiful pea-green
nut

the toil of swelling to bursting
swelling and bursting

each time a long ache
but willingly borne

joyous muchness!

shake a ripe oak
and you'll hear
strange music
like far-off maracas

a fruiting oak
is like an outburst of words
you might say
lyric

hold an acorn in your palm to see its shine
like well-loved furniture

and how it fulfils the tiny chalice
which is rough and seemingly unfinished

the cup partakes of the nature of the tree
being workaday and built to last

and the nut is the pearl of great price
bearer of a secret code

which is the singularity of an oak
alone in a field

a child puts an acorn in a glass of water
  to watch the little boat tip over
  – and again!

a child pokes an acorn from its cup and sips
  mummy at my party I am
  having a little drink of oak
and makes of the green nut
a toy for a toy

a child keeps an acorn in a matchbox
  to see what hatches out

a child puts an acorn under her pillow
  to see what dreams will come

the oak makes of itself a storehouse
wealth beyond worth

to be dropped into the lap
of the meadow it grew out of

and the ground will crunch and crack
underfoot like an expensive driveway

and the oak will feel a certain hopeless
lightness

a mast year takes it out of an oak
and to show for it only
a few little ones

carried off and planted
by a loud bird with tweezers for a beak

the rest just left lying about
food for thought
(the waste of it)

old man
enough is never enough
old tree you can stop

7

and this is the seventh part
which is the last and most strange

a number that has a limping quality
and is full of echoes and marvellous corridors

a number not worn away by maths
but polished into lastingness

seven tells us something will happen
that we have not foreseen

or that was entirely to be expected
and both will have a meaning

and because we are close to an ending
we must warn you to expect

anything

for seven is the number of the angels and trumpets
and also of the final thunders

behold the qualities of a very old oak
mightiness
quirkiness
a certain kingly hauteur
as in one who's seen it all before

old meaning *of the past*
of long ago
and not meaning *any old how*
which is not the way
an oak tree makes its life

old timer
with something to say
to Jack-o'-the-Woods
a word or two
on the subject of hiding

Jack who never grew out of mischief
in his turban of leaves
and his leaf-beard
you might almost think him wise
expert in nodding and head-scratching

> *Jack-o'-the-Woods*
> *Jack-up-to-no-good*
> *Jack-laugh-in-your-face*
> *Jack-spit-in-your-face*

that part of an oak beyond alteration
the crux that holds true
is the heartwood
the very dry old wood
which is also the deadwood

stand under an oak's rafters
to notice the work
the sureness of effort

like a string quartet
whose players have no need
to look at the score
or each other

if there's the odd branch broken off
its raw blunt end is only
a relic of a suffering

almost forgotten
and no longer to the point

a very old oak
has no need for explanations

these days the oak holds close to its heart a nest of bats
(the birds long gone)
and finds comfort in the scuffly scratchings
the upside-down stretchings
and bare-faced bickerings

the oak is not yet dead
but is beset by gushes of fern
and rain's deep scourings
and by beefsteak fungus
like a drooping orange tutu
memory of dancing

the oak is like a hot compost
from which this or that living thing
might crawl or spring or flap

you might say the oak is
dying of kindness

an oak of great age has gravitas
like a baroque cathedral
and must be painted by a famous artist
at dawn and noon and in the afternoon and at dusk

or chips of bark must be taken from it as souvenirs

or it must be knocked on for luck

or it must be crawled into by two small boys
making spooky noises
so the oak appears
to be itself a howling ghost

the half-life is that which persists
after the full-life has gone

a way of looking at the world
from the acute angle of having
not much time

and the words that come to mind
are *stone* and *woe*

darkness suits an old oak
which is a galleon tilting in the moonlight
like a Doré engraving

washed up in every sense of the word
an *objet trouvé*
both strange and everyday

and the bats are black smuts
drawing imaginary lines
round and around

so they know where to come back to

this is the time for a very old oak to look back
to its heyday of flexing in the wind
of tossing birds up into the air
and catching them again
of flourishing greenly
and of the great meadow blowing
(cheery heads of knapweed cranesbill thistle)
of the lovely washing rain
of the last leaves coppering and dropping
making a sound like cutlery

easy then to be alive
and oh so very ordinary

one day a lackadaisical thrush
will wipe her beak on a topmost twig

something will stick and tickle its way
into the bark
and into the sapwood
enough for a little life to hang by

thus mistletoe will make itself a home
and take unto its tangly self
those things that uphold a tree

come back after years to find an oak
like a scarecrow with its stuffing hanging out

and this is the first manner of dying

or picture an oak with a wound
freckled with spores
which arrived on the wind in no time

not the kindly milk-cap family
with their dreamy listening
but one with its own good in mind

the slow work of fungus
threading its fibres
softly into the greenwood
softly into the heartwood

eating the trunk from the outside in
with the patience of a miner or a seamstress
eating the trunk from the inside out
to make of the heart a powdery ruin

for the heart is not a stronghold
the heart is not a stone

and this is the second manner of dying

in the weakness of age an oak
may fall victim to windthrow

what is happening now
is that the bald branches
are more heavy than the trunk can bear

an east wind will rake and rake
at the hoary old head
throwing off twigs like peelings or parings
and from under the ground will arise
a sound of tearing and wrenching
as the root-hairs and the small roots and the great sinker root
are twisted and pulled from the good earth that loved them

a hold is loosed
a bond is broken

and this is the third manner of dying

or an oak may simply outlive its own vigour

the topmost branches
lost for leaves
jangle like antlers
bric-a-brac of tree-death

picture the oak like a sea at ebb tide
cringing back from its edges
to leave only the gist

which is the trunk
and the sinker root
and the slow slow-beating heart

come back after years
to find an oak like a buddha
squatly lost in thought or memory

and somewhere across the meadow
a sapling like a tiny helicopter
amid the heads of knapweed cranesbill thistle
flapping its new green wings

which may be a comfort to one
sans teeth, sans eyes, sans taste, sans everything

who knows if an oak can let itself rest
or if its desire is entirely other
or if its desire is nothing at all

at last the oak must give up its ghost
must crumble and flake
and splinter and creak
until with a roar it is brought to its knees

a great slumping
as when a poacher brings down a rhino

the oak will suddenly find itself lowly
and look up at the sky
at the birds swiftly passing
and will hunker down like a hare to her form

and at the last end
the oak will find itself regarded
by the tremulous grasses
by the clean white owl and by brown owl
and by the singing bats
and by Woodpecker who will not laugh
and by Pip the Robin who may flick-flicker for a moment
and by the gaudy thankless flowers of the meadow
(not what you could have called companions)

plantain
thistle
knapweed
orchid
cranesbill
sorrel
bird's-foot trefoil

and Light will mean nothing
and Air will mean nothing
and Rain will mean nothing

and an oak must think nothing
and an oak must feel nothing
but a long vanishment into the earth

and all this may take years

Notes & Acknowledgements

First and foremost thank you to Andy, Bluebell and Daisy for your love and enthusiasm and for making it easy for me to find time to write. This book wouldn't be here without you. Thank you also to my sisters Judy and Susie who have been tirelessly encouraging over the years.

I'm grateful to the friends who were early readers – John Beatty, Sasha Dugdale, Rachel Genn, Conor O'Callaghan, Mary Peace and Jacob Polley. Your encouragement helped me keep going when I was doubting. I'm also grateful to the merry band of poets at the Northern Poetry Workshop for the good times and the sharp ears and eyes.

A huge thank you to my editor Don Paterson who sees things in a poem that even the poem hasn't noticed.

And finally I must thank the very tiny stone outhouse in our garden, which was my writing room. I know how lucky I am to have somewhere I can close the door.